Rebel MLM :

No B.S. Guide to Attracting High Quality Prospects and Sponsoring More Reps with Almost NO Rejections

by Richard Williams

Copyright © 2014

Table of Contents

Acknowledgement

I am grateful to my close friend and my uplines who signed me up in this wonderful industry.

This book is dedicated to the marketing excellence of Perry Marshall, Mike Dillard, Tim Erway, Eben Pagan, Frank Kern, Daegan Smith, Ray Higdon, Eric Worre, David Wood, Todd Falcone, Ben Settle, Mark Wieser, Tim Sales, Russell Brunson, Ryan Deiss, Jordan Adler, Glen Livingston, Terry Dean, Andre Chaperon, Bob Burg & Robert Blackman.

Bonus

These strategies, I learned from Tim Ferriss, the author of "**4 Hour Workweek**". You can use it anywhere including your MLM to supercharge your results and duplication.

Interest and energy are cyclical.

If you want to build your MLM working 16 hours a day every single day for next 5 years, would you do it?

Of course not.

Instead you will find better ways to reduce those 16 hours into 5-6 hours and still outproduce.

Work only towards producing maximum results, being more productive and effective.

Less is not laziness.

Doing less meaningless work is not laziness. Many network marketers waste their time in activities like chitchatting, facebooking, checking their emails, gossiping, sharpening the pencils.

When they get some time out of it, they do prospecting, doing the presentations or closings.

And they wonder how some people building the business part time surpass them. Focus on being effective and productive than being busy.

Timing is never right.

For all the important things, timing always sucks. There is no good time to start in MLM industry; there is no good time to go full time in MLM. Conditions are never perfect.

Emphasize Strengths, Don't Fix Weaknesses.

Most people are good at a handful of things and utterly miserable at most. I am great at online lead generation and marketing but terrible at calling the leads, fixing appointments. My upline does it for me.

In your team, find out each other's strength and leverage on it.

If your upline is great at 3-way calls, bring more prospects during those calls. If your downline is great at doing face to face presentation and you are not, then let him handle that part and help him fixing the part where he sucks. e.g lead generation.

If you want to become successful in MLM, you have to take advantage of strengths of your team-mates.

If you just follow just this tip, it will be worth the investment in this book.

1. My Story

The first thing you should know about me is I am not a millionaire.

I am not a PhD in network marketing.

I am not a network marketing guru or expert.

I am just an ordinary guy with kickass marketing skills that helps me to do a lot of things.

I have failed more times than I succeeded. I learnt many things the hard way. I tried several approaches which don't work, found out some which work through trial and error.

I tried some approaches which I thought would never work but worked fabulously and some approaches which I thought would work were severely bombed.

There are a lot of people running and claiming that they have all the answers. I don't proclaim that I have all the answers for you but whatever answers I have are pretty important.

You shouldn't just believe whatever I say, infact I suggest you to go through my material with healthy scepticism and scientific perspective and put the ideas to use and see for yourself how great they work.

This book _won't_ make you successful or rich, thinking something outside yourself to make yourself successful is a pathetic approach.

Whatever you need to succeed is already in you. This book will only help you to acquire some new skills.

If you want to work on yourself, I will suggest you to get this book **"Psychocybernetics"** by Dr. Maxwell Maltz

In this book, I will talk about all the approaches you can use but a small warning before you go through them.

WARNING: This book is not a be-all and end-all solution for Network Marketing. All the approaches I talk about *won't* work for everybody. There will be some approaches which would work absolutely great for you and some approaches would work terribly bad, that doesn't mean it's a useless approach. It just means that this approach is not suitable for you. It all depends upon your personality, your work ethics, your background, your work experience.

Now before I dive into the nitty gritty, I wanted to share a few things about myself which I believe you will find important.

First everyone sucks in the beginning, I did for long time and even my upline did, but many of them never bothered to mention it.

They just *casually forgot to go over that little piece of info*, and many of them never bothered to mention that.

I got started in this industry just after I lost my hope to get into good MBA college after *1 year of job and 1 year of failed attempt at MBA preparation.*

Exactly on my birthday, I was recruited by my closest friend.

This was a massive, hugely uncomfortable stretch for me.

He tried to convince me for 1 year in vain but I didn't join it for some personal reasons as I wanted to try my luck at MBA which didn't yield any stellar results except few converts here and there.

Eventually, I signed up with him after he followed up with me for long time.

When I got started, I had very little self confidence and was close to dead broke. I used to drive my upline mad with endless questions and someone who would do whatever to avoid calling my prospects. Maybe you can relate.

But I "*saw the circles*" and grasped the potential, and my little world was greatly expanded as we traveled from my home to some very posh areas.

I hanged out with a lot of people from corporate, from traditional businesses and many more people like me, who believed that the future of the world lies in this powerful "new" concept of Network Marketing.

The short version of that story is that I was completely '*sold out*' or rather completely brainwashed , did whatever they told me to do, I bought whatever they told me to buy, I went to every small and big event possible and dug in deep till I went into debt. I couldn't attend some big events because I had very little or no money left with me.

Still I had the persistence of Saddam Hussein.

In a long span of 18 months, I traveled a couple hundred miles and did hundreds of presentations with my uplines and on my own.

In fact I even went through a dry spell where I got 126 NO's in a row.

No No No No No No No No No No No No No No No No No No No No
No No No No No No No No No No No No No No No No No No No No
No No No No No No No No No No No No No No No No No No No No
No No No No No No No No No No No No No No No No No No No No
No No No No No No No No No No No No No No No No No No No No
No No No No No No No No No No No No No No No No No No No No
No No No No No No No No No No No.

I know. It doesn't sound like much or it doesn't look that bad on paper but for me it felt like NO^{126}.

I did almost all things my uplines told me to do, system told me to do.

I devised all kinds of clever ways to contact people that most network marketers would never think of, let alone try. (Some of them are just embarrassing to share)

When I used to ask my uplines, why it is not working for me, they used to either tell me that **"You just need to do more of it"** or **"It's just a numbers game**." or **"You just need to show more plans."** and no matter how hard I tried, everything just turned out to be a utter disaster for me.

"If you are failing at something, it means only two things either you are doing something wrong or you are not doing something enough."

Some of my crosslines who were **"successful"** in the eyes of the society used to make me feel embarrassed in front of everybody asking me about **"How much money I was making?"** and although I was showing a lot of plans than 95% of the crowd, I had no results to show.

And after trying different things quite unsuccessfully, slowly and relentlessly, I proved to myself that no matter how I attempted to do this, it wasn't going to work the way my upline told me to do or system told me to do.

As I saw heavy duty attrition rate in system itself. People with 6 months & younger occupied 70% of seats. People with 12 months or less occupied 90% and remaining seats were occupied by people who were more than 12 moths.

Every month of coffee shop, traveling expense in that business became a bigger ball and chain of failure, mounting evidence of my ineffectiveness that eventually became impossible to ignore.

Agony-----Pain------Extreme Brokeness

I labored under a burden of inner agony, maddening frustration and desperation. I wondered to myself how anybody could possibly explain or justify such a long, uninterrupted string of failure.

My greatest fear was that the prospect at my next meeting would ask me how much money I was making. I developed elaborate mechanisms in my presentations, just to prevent this question from ever getting asked and I learned exclusive methods to deflect that question skilfully.

"People want to succeed. They want to do a good job. They don't like to turn out lousy work. If your people are consistently failing, it's not their fault – it's your system's fault." W. Edwards Deming

Did that statement hit me like a ton of bricks?

No, not at the time.

Actually it slowly melted its way down through my brain like a hot steel ingot on a frozen lake. Every time they would tell us about how the system is flawless but still I could see most people quitting. I am not crying foul here. I don't have to.

Whenever they said

"*We are the product of the system. The System is the secret, the system fails not.*"

I would look around and see the 99% failure rate and be reminded that someone must surely be jesting.

So I decided to keep aside the advice which was not serving me or most of the crowd anymore and I was determined to find answers on my own and this book is the result of those efforts I made.

When I started, we had no tools for making our life easier.

Only coffee shop meetings or home meetings. And mostly at the plush places, so the prospects coming there should get that higher class feel.

People were traveling from long places, driving long way to get to that coffee shop to show a single plan or meet his/her upline. Nobody complained about it. Even when that long mileage was piling up to become a huge stone of failure.

Some did continue despite seeing any long lasting results, most of them quit. Some never bothered to come only. They lost in translation.

For all my hard work, I had nothing to show for it but debt, an abundance of products and a dwindling list of friends who actually still talked with me.

The biggest epiphany I had is when I started dabbling and started learning about marketing, sales, copywriting, because I saw if I continue doing what I was doing for next 20 years, it's not going to give me any more results.

And I began looking for real answers to why I was spinning my wheels.

So I looked at the part which was not working and when I did, my entire view of this business changed forever.

I have written this book because I don't want everyone else to suffer just because they don't have the effective methods of prospecting, presenting and closing.

2. How to Develop Bulletproof Mindset?

If you want to succeed in MLM, your mindset holds the key.

It's very essential to develop the bulletproof mindset before you start your prospecting, presenting, closing activities.

Develop a daily ritual of activities. Schedule specific time for prospecting, presenting, blogging.

Do highest priority activities first. Don't check your email first.

Use most of your time for prospecting, presenting & team building and spend less time in useless activities like gossiping, chitchatting, facebooking or checking emails.

Use a planner and stick to it.

Work more on your business than in your business.

When working in the business, do the activities, which produce the highest results.

Use this tool, **Rescue Time**

Be grateful and learn to appreciate things.

Associate with right kind of people.

3. How to dissolve your greatest emotional blocks using simple pen, paper and pad ?

Before you start applying the principles I am going to teach you, you should go through this process atleast once. If you don't, certain things will happen

1. You many not complete this book
2. You may find some techniques, strategies wrong and totally misfit even if they are not
3. You may not take any action or you may take very little action
4. You may not get any results or you may get negative results in the worst case

Emotions are everything.

We buy with emotions and justify with logic.

Whatever problems, challenges you are facing, whatever limiting beliefs you have, whatever pain you are having can be completely eliminated through this.

This is such a powerful method for authentic manifestation.

It's not about feel good factor.

It's not about Secret, Magic, Thinking Big, affirmations or any motivation stuff.

It's about clearing your inner garbage that is holding you back.

You should absolutely consume this information, internalize it and see the real magic happening.

Thoughts create our life.

You can think about something until you are blue in the face and not have a single thing happen because of it.

Your thoughts can definitely put you in the right mental and emotional state to create something, however, so they serve as a strong foundation for the overall process.

By placing yourself into the proper emotional state, you will bring into focus what you want.

The better you can make yourself feel emotionally on a regular basis, the more quickly you will progress towards attaining what you seek.

Your thoughts are constantly running in the background, no matter what you are doing. Much of the time you are not even aware of them because they occur automatically based on what you see, hear, feel and believe.

Like most other people, you probably spend the majority of your time focusing your attention out toward the things you see, hear and experience moment to moment. Only when you start thinking consciously do you become aware of your thoughts.

For example, when you are trying to solve a problem you may become aware of your inner voice saying things like this: "**What if I tried another approach to this problem? Or maybe I should just ask someone his/her opinion; he/she has a lot of knowledge about this type of thing.**" As you puzzle out various options, your thoughts will inspire different actions that can help you resolve the issue.

You may also become aware of your thoughts when you are trying to remember something.

Being able to tune into your thoughts this way can be a big help because it shakes you out of the mindless habits you formed to make your life easier.

This sense of being on "autopilot" can be very helpful at times, but it can also make you feel like a brainless zombie.

Being disconnected from your thoughts can also cause problems by making you a victim of your own emotions. Remember that your thoughts trigger your emotions.

If you are not aware of your thoughts, you will find yourself experiencing wildly fluctuating emotions without any idea why.

Perhaps you can remember instances when your mood seemed to shift dramatically for no apparent reason. You were feeling fine and then all of a sudden, you were angry, sad or depressed.

Most likely, unbeknownst to you, your thoughts began moving in an unproductive direction, triggering corresponding emotions.

The same thing can happen due to external influences also. Think about the last time your mood was affected because of one little thing that someone else said or did.

Like if someone was rude to you for no apparent reason, feelings of anger and defensiveness may have flared up, effectively ruining the good mood you were enjoying just minutes before.

However, there is also a more positive side to this process. Just as your thoughts can trigger emotions, your emotions can serve as an excellent indicator of what types of thoughts you've been thinking. If you find yourself feeling angry, helpless, hopeless, or stressed much of the time, you know you may need to work on your thoughts in order to make them more positive.

In order to change your thoughts, you first have to become aware of what they are now. This involves simply turning your attention inward as often as possible. Several times throughout the day, remember to pause and pay attention to what is happening within you.

Do a mental check and consider:

1. How do you feel?
2. Which emotions are you experiencing right now?
3. What direction are your thoughts going in right now?
4. Are you being pessimistic or optimistic?
5. Are you expecting the best or worst?
6. Are you allowing outer circumstances to negatively affect you?

You may find it helpful to keep a small journal or notebook nearby while you practice tuning into your thoughts and emotions throughout the day.

If you notice yourself feeling or thinking negatively, ask yourself what brought it on.

1. Did something happen?
2. Or were you just feeling frustrated about something?
3. Were you worrying about something?

Keep detailed notes about WHEN and WHY you tend to slip into negative thinking/feeling, and you'll be much more aware of the patterns you need to change.

One of your biggest challenges will probably be remembering to check in at all. You may be so used to letting your thoughts and emotions run automatically that you keep forgetting to monitor them.

If it helps, try putting up notes in strategic locations. Put one in your workspace, on the dashboard of your car, on the bathroom mirror, the refrigerator, etc.

The notes can display any message you want, but try something simple like, "**Time to check in**," or "**How do you feel?**" When your eyes fall on these notes, you'll remember to pause and pay attention to your thoughts and feelings.

When you first begin the process of monitoring your thoughts and feelings, you may be tempted to tell some "**white lies**" You may try telling yourself that you're feeling fine, even though you may feel annoyed or pressured. You may not really "feel" anything at all when you check in, so you'll fib in your journal that you feel good. Avoid this at all costs.

If you are serious about wanting to conquer your negative thinking habits, these little fibs will not do you any good. You cannot cheat your way into positive thinking. If it's not genuine, it won't create the lasting changes you want. Be sure to always be honest with yourself.

If you are feeling angry, acknowledge it. If you are feeling bored, let it be okay to be bored.

Remember that this process is not about covering up or denying your emotions. When you refuse to process emotions, they will keep coming back to haunt you until you process and release them.

Contrary to popular belief, negative feelings are not harmful or "bad" in any way. The only bad thing about them is what we choose to do with them most of the time: either express them in destructive ways, or ignore them so they keep controlling us.

Do yourself a huge favour: **HONOR YOUR FEELINGS**. Don't try to convince yourself that you shouldn't feel the way you are feeling. Don't try to squash down negative feelings because you don't know how to handle them. Instead, deal with them when they come up.

Allow yourself to feel the feelings, work through the thoughts that pop up in your mind, and then let go of the issue so it doesn't continue to bother you. The magnitude of each issue you face will ultimately determine how quickly you can get through this process.

Minor annoyances can probably be processed and released in minutes. Big heartaches, betrayals, or rejections may take a little more time.

As you work through these feelings, pay close attention to any underlying beliefs they may trigger.

You may initially get angry about one small situation, but trigger memories of other unresolved experiences that make this current situation seem much worse. If your emotions seem excessive or disproportionate to the current situation, you may have some old beliefs that are being aggravated.

This sounds like a bad thing but only if you don't address it. That's why journaling can be so helpful in a process like this.

When you start recording your feelings and noticing how certain beliefs are triggered, you become aware of a limiting belief that you now have the power to change.

When you first begin monitoring your thoughts and feelings, you might find yourself at a loss about how to change them. You should honour your feelings and work through them. You may be wondering at what point you should "change" a negative thought or feeling, or if you should change them at all.

It can get confusing at times, but it really depends on the situation. There will usually be two possible scenarios:

<u>Know When to Let Go</u>

If you find yourself feeling badly because you are stuck on some minor issue that doesn't really matter in the grand scheme of things, it's a good idea to change your thinking and bring up some more positive emotions. Obsessing over something so inconsequential won't do you any good; it will only keep you mired in a cycle of negativity.

For this type of situation, you will simply need to make a choice to let it go and turn your thoughts in a more positive direction. You might find yourself losing focus quite frequently at the beginning. You might turn your thoughts away from aggravation, only to find yourself fuming again a few minutes later. That's okay; just be persistent in choosing to let it go again, and again, and again – no matter how many times you have to do it.

If you keep practicing this technique daily, you will eventually develop the ability to control your focus like you wouldn't believe.

Not only will it help you control negative thoughts and generate more positive ones, it can also help you in all other areas of your life.

Know When to Process Emotions

Now, for the situations that are bigger and more troubling, I do not suggest trying to ignore those without processing the emotions involved. As I described previously, *"processing"* emotions means simply allowing yourself to feel them, work through them, and let them go when the time is right.

How long it takes to process them will be completely up to you. Big disappointments and heartaches will obviously take longer than smaller upsets.

There is a fine line between giving yourself time to honour your feelings and wallowing in misery. If you find yourself lingering too long on the dark side, take out your journal and explore the reasons for it.

1. Do your negative emotions serve a deeper purpose?
2. Are you afraid to let go of them and move on?
3. What do you think will happen if you stopped brooding?

Speaking of journaling, this is a good time to mention that your journal can serve as a very effective purging platform. One of the reasons why your emotions often hold you hostage is because you don't let them out. You bottle them up inside and keep stressing over them.

Think about the last time you felt really angry or stressed about something and you poured it all out to a good friend. After you finished spilling the whole terrible story, didn't you feel relieved? That's because in the process of telling your story you were processing your emotions and getting them out of your mind and heart.

Your journal can serve the same purpose, but even better. Instead of censoring yourself or holding back details you wouldn't share with anyone else, you can spill them out in all their gory detail in your journal.

You can swear your heart out, stab the paper with your pen, and completely vent your emotions without worrying about offending anyone. It's very freeing.

If your anger or frustration involves another person, you can also use this method to write them a letter and give them a piece of your mind.

When you first begin using this activity regularly, you may struggle to fully connect with your negative emotions, especially if you have developed a habit of squashing them down and disconnecting from them.

If so, I urge you to practice, practice, and practice some more. The only way you are going to reconnect with your emotions is to keep trying to tap into them and honour them when they come up.

You may also be surprised to notice a generous serving of fear rising up whenever you think about processing your emotions. This is very common for people who were shamed or ridiculed about emotional displays during childhood, or even for people who just got used to blocking their emotions.

Once you push through this fear, you will realize that there is nothing scary there. Your emotions won't overwhelm you and they won't eat you alive. They are just feelings. They come and go.

They grow in intensity, and then fade away again. If you have genuine difficulty expressing your emotions, you might find it worthwhile to consult a therapist or counselor. They are trained to help you work through painful or unsettling emotions safely and compassionately.

Learning to work with your thoughts and emotions is a process that will take time.

Don't expect yourself to master it immediately. Understand that you will get better at it the longer you do it, and be patient with the process.

Think of it this way: even one positive thought or feeling a day puts you farther ahead than you were before. Take it one step at a time and be sure to celebrate small victories as you go along.

If you want to learn more advanced methods I would recommend

www.theemotioncode.com
www.crackyouregg.com
www.tappingsolution.com

4. 4 Critical Phases of Network Marketing

There are four critical phases in Network Marketing.

First phase : Unconscious Incompetence

This phase lasts for first 6 months. This is the phase where 65-70 % of newly signed up people fizzle out. In this stage, people are very excited, they just got signed up but they don't know what to do. They are like a new fish in the pond, if they are not trained or coached properly, they are highly likely to quit the business.

It's that phase where people don't know what they don't know.

Second phase : Conscious Incompetence

This is the phase where people know what they don't know. This phase lasts from 6 months to 18 months. In this phase, if you stick with your upline and company, you go through a lot of challenges, hardships, you build a sizable team but your income is not at the same level you want it to be. It's the phase where around 20-30 % people quit the business. Some of your downlines will stop attending training & events, stop doing activities, stop doing business altogether.

Third phase : Conscious Competence

This is the phase where you know what you know. Your income is growing on autopilot. Your team is growing, you are asked to come on stage to share your journey, you are also asked to give the trainings. This is the phase where around 3-5% people quit the business. In this phase you have to hold hand of one active and growing upline who can take you to the next level.

Fourth phase : Unconscious

Competence

This is the phase when whatever you do happens on unconscious level, nobody has to tell you about what to do, how to act in certain situations. It's the phase where whatever you are doing is effortless/elegant. This is the phase where you are one of the top earners. You are managing big teams, you are handling leaders on your teams.

If you are successful in Network Marketing, you have probably gone through all these phases. You can't skip any of these phases; you have to go through all of them in the same fashion.

5. How to Approach Family and Friends without harming your reputation and straining your relationships?

1. **Don't mislead your friends by introducing your product or business as If you were recommending a restaurant or movie.**

   Most new network marketers do what their upline tell them to do "Just talk to your friends. It's like recommending a restaurant or movie."

   But is it? How many friends has anyone lost you recommending a restaurant or movie?

   How many friends have been lost recommending network marketing?

   It's like you meet your friends at lunch or coffee, you exchange news and pleasantries but the tension and anxiety set when you start talking about your MLM venture. Your friends doesn't like saying "NO" to you and you don't feel comfortable revealing your hidden agenda at the end asking them to buy.

   That's why the recruiters continue recruiting, leaving in their wake millions who have lost money and self-esteem and no place to go for Christmas Dinner or Friend Reunion.

2. **Warn them up front that you're selling what you are going to talk about.**

   If you do this with sincerity and without apology, most friends will at least give you their ear and they won't feel betrayed at the end. They might even give you a referral or two.

Friends often recommend things to each other, and no one expects their friend to be selling what they recommend. To act and talk as if it's a regular recommendation from one friend to another, and then surprise them at the end with "**Oh, I sell it**" is a guaranteed trust buster.

The feeling of having been snuck up on and used is what strains the friendship, not the fact that you're a marketer.

To act and talk as if it's a regular recommendation from one friend to another, and then surprise them at the end with "**Oh, trustbuster.**"

Here's a way to introduce your thing to your friend without losing their trust. Before you say anything about your product or business, you're immediately transparent:

"Hey John, I have this new thing I'm selling because I finally lost some weight with it, and I have to tell you about it…"

Now you've told your friend up front that you're selling the thing you're going to talk about.

3. **Don't ask your friends to buy. Ask for a referral instead.**

It's hard for some people to say "**NO**" to a salesperson, especially a friend. So they say **Maybe**.

And you hope; you call back, but in vain. They see you on caller ID and don't pick up anymore.

To prevent this, don't ask for the sale, ever. Ask for the referral instead. Here's a way to do it:

Assume you've used the opener above: "**Say John, I have this new thing I'm selling because I finally lost some weight with it, and I have to tell you about it.**" [John cringes.]

Smile and continue: "**In case you know anyone** [pause, to allow his brain to take in that you're not hitting him up] **who might want to know about a product like that. Ok?** [Pause for John's reply.]

Instant relief. His brain might even light up and think of someone. You haven't abused his trust, and he might even spend a little time thinking about whom he might know who might want to buy from you, his trusted friend still. He'll probably even think of you whenever any of his friends ask him about weight loss—because he knows you won't pressure his friends either.

Asking a friend to buy is like bopping them over the head. Friends want to help their friends.

They feel bad when they can't. Give them a chance to help by asking for the referral, never the sale.

4. **Don't ask your friends to sell. Ask for a referral instead.**

Don't listen to uplines who demand that you "Make your list of 100 closest contacts and start calling to share this wonderful and amazing business opportunity with them" They're asking you to trade in the friendships you have built over decades for a few quick bucks.

Friends want to believe that this might be it. Then they fail. That's when they feel abused. They trusted, bought in, then discovered that they can't sell. They get mad at themselves, then they get mad at you.

"I can't believe I let you talk me into this. I must have had a stupid moment."

They trusted, bought in, and then discovered that they can't sell. They get mad at themselves, then they got mad at you.

Instead, ask for a referral to someone who loves to sell: **"Do you know anyone who likes to sell and who might be looking for something like this?"**

Then let go. If they want to sell, they'll ask. Then you can show them what's involved, without pressuring them or offering dubious promises of riches if they buy in.

And never ask a customer to sell, either. They're like everyone else—most don't want to sell.

You can ask for referrals.

There is a method to ask for a referral from existing product customers, you can learn it in subsequent chapters.

5. **Lead with your own hot button.**

Dispense with second-guessing them, overcoming objections, mind control, scare tactics, or other persuasion techniques.

Sales people are supposed to sell; so, they're always thinking about ways to get people to buy.

Every company believes its products are the greatest and that they're the best in the history of the world. "Everyone wants these products, they sell themselves" companies promise their tens of thousands of sales recruits. If people aren't buying, it must be that the sales people don't know how to sell.

So, the folks learn how to find people's hot buttons, overcome their objections, and create fear of loss— everything they can to persuade those people to buy. After a few rejections, especially from friends or family, the once enthusiastic marketer loses self-esteem and quits.

Instead of trying to sell everyone you know, why not find those who might already be looking for what you sell? No need to persuade anyone.

Lead with your hot button, so that people whose buttons match yours can find you.

When you lead with your hot button, you're speaking with authenticity. Who knows better than you what turns you on? You don't have to feign enthusiasm. It bubbles over. The task is to reign it in.

You don't have to scheme to get your friends or anyone else to buy. Instead, bring to consciousness why you love your product, why you decided to start selling it.

Why you keep on doing your business, no matter how hard it is to keep slogging. This is your hot button, your why. And it's a reflection of who you already are.

6. **Enthusiasm sells. Hype and Hounding don't.**

Don't tell them how great your thing is.

The greater you say your thing is, the more suspect and desperate you look. Remember, they know you're selling it and will make money if they buy. Tell your hot button story.

Then let the authentic tale and referral magic do their work on like minded people.

7. **Recommend the smallest package, like a prudent advisor.**

   Imagine your friend is interested in starting their business with you and it's time to buy inventory.

   They often ask how much you started with. Tell them the truth, whatever it is. Even if you started with the biggest deluxe package, surprise them.

   "You don't have to start with the biggest one. Maybe the starter package is the best one for you. Tell me how you would use the product and we can see if that's the best option. You can always buy more later."

   What do you think they expect a seller to recommend—the biggest or the smallest? Your recommendation tells your friend you're still a friend, advising them rather than preying on them.

After close friends and family, there comes a warm market. Most people do wrong type of invitations to their warm market and that's why they get pretty much rejections. These are some keys to warm market success.

1. Be yourself: Don't reinvent the wheel. When you try to be someone else to your warm market, these people will shy away. They won't be attentive to what you are going to say. Instead be yourself, talk to them as you will do normally. Tell them that you are exploring a business opportunity at this time and you want them to take a look at it and you don't care whether they are interested in it or not.

2. Be excited and enthusiastic: If you act excited and enthusiastic, people will be more attentive to what you want to say. They will be more open to receive information.

3. Don't confuse invitation with presentation: Don't try to present opportunity on the phone or in the person at the time of inviting. The key to inviting is telling as little information as possible in order to increase curiosity, not to raise defences. Don't try to act professional with your friends. Always give them two options while inviting.

4. Confirm 24 hours before: Call them 24 hours in advance to get confirmation from them. So if their appointment is not confirmed, then you can schedule other appointment at the same time without wasting your time and you can reschedule that appointment at some later stage.

6. How to re-approach burnt out warm market?

If you have failed at other MLMs , then probably you must be facing this problem.

The reason is you don't want to bother your friends, family and relatives because of your previous failures.

There was an industry veteran when asked when you should approach your family and friends, without blinking an eye he said

"When you don't care if they will sign up or not."

What you have to do is qualify them fast.

Asking them open ended questions, collect their response and move on. Don't go into argumentative and convincing mode if they are not open.

So approach them with utmost honesty, if they say "NO", change the topic and ask for referral.

Ask them "Do you anyone who can benefit from this opportunity or from the products/services?"

There is another way which will help you to heal your strained relationship

1. Apologize: Reach out to them without any agenda. Talk to them. Apologize to them saying, "I clearly made you uncomfortable. I did it wrong. I am sorry if I made you feel awkward. If it has strained our relationship, I don't want that. I was overwhelmed with passion. I got excited for what I thought would be a good future for you and for me but I clearly overdid it and I am sorry."

2. Real Goal: Your real goal should not be trying to recruit each and every friend and family member. Your real goal should be to educate them about your business and let them take their own decision. Don't be the person who push, call and harass everybody.

   Your goal is not to get them. Your goal is education.

3. Interact without inviting: Don't tell them about your opportunity, let them ask. Call them without agenda. Call them just to say "Hi"

4. Understanding & Education: Tell them upfront that, you are not asking them a favour, you are not telling them to involve. Friendship is more important than business.

5. Emotional Deposit: If you have approached them in a wrong way, you have depleted emotional bank account in their banks. You have depleted it by pushing, pursuing them. Try to build that emotional bank account by taking genuine interest in them and offering help to them.

6. Publicly use your product: But don't talk about it, don't turn it into the pitch.

7. Talk about results without prospecting: If while communication, if you get chance to talk, talk about benefits of the product. Don't turn it into prospecting event. If they ask you, go soft, don't try to pitch them.

8. Be a real friend and family member: Talk and behave the way you are. Always think what you can do for them.

7. How to create professional rolodex of contacts without cold-calling ever?

LinkedIn is a very good medium for prospecting medium if prospecting is done right. It's much better and faster to get in touch with more qualified prospects than facebook *if done right* without having to do cold calls forever. I learned this strategy from my friend who sponsored dozens of people using LinkedIn he didn't know earlier.

But some people use it horribly and irresponsibly. Most of them don't know how to use it at all.

So let's learn about LinkedIn Shenanigan Tactics

1. **Group Hijacking**: Go to a group and posting there about your opportunity in words most people can't figure out and then lure them to show the presentation.

   Attack in the Dark: Send invite to unknown people without introducing yourself and then spam them with your opportunity over their head instead of building rapport and relationship. Directly asking someone whether he or she is open to take a look at their business.

2. **Dubious Profile:** Vague and inexplicable profile on LinkedIn which doesn't say anything about you but full of fluff.

3. **Cold Calling Monster Fury Unleashed**: Cold calling people from your connections and asking them whether they are open for any opportunity without asking them any questions or building any rapport.

   If you are using some of these tricks, it will backfire on you.

In fact, there are better ways to connect and build true connection with them.

1. When you connect with someone make sure your profile looks professional and not amateurish.

2. Take some time to write about you, your work experience in detail. Don't use words like wonderful, opportunity, multi-million dollar, visionary, ground floor etc etc.

3. Use professional looking photo.

4. When you connect with someone, introduce yourself properly and tell them why you are connecting with them.

There are ways to start the conversation.

Dos and Don'ts

1. Don't talk about your business in the first message unless asked specifically.

2. Don't ask for cell no in first message, generally it's shared on their profile.

3. Even if you have their mobile Nos, don't directly contact or call them. Build rapport first through personal messages.

4. After exchanging 4-5 messages, give them the hint at either you would be connecting with them over that weekend or any specified day.

5. They will be much more comfortable that way and will recognize your voice.

6. In first talk, try to learn more about them; don't bring the business if not required. Try to set up a meeting once, if prospects are local. (That will increase the closing ratio.)

7. If the person is showing a lot of interest, then just ask him a couple of open ended questions and either send him to third party presentation or invite him to come and see what you have to offer. Give him two options, it will increase turnout ratio.

8. How to use Government's loophole to sign up more people?

Home-based businesses are quickly becoming the fastest growing form of business startups. Growing your business out of your home allows for flexibility that is difficult when renting or buying office and warehouse space. Although working at home requires self-discipline, the benefits can be substantial - especially in the start-up years.

1. More Work Time, Less Commute Time

According to a recent Gallup poll, Americans spend an average of almost 50 minutes a day commuting to and from their offices. One of the best benefits of working in a home office is that commuting involves no more than a few steps to the spare room or the basement. That leaves more time for revenue-producing activities.

2. The Ability to Scale Up or Scale Down Quickly

When you rent or own office space, the size of your business is fixed to the size of the space. In the event where downsizing makes sense, you may not be able to do so quickly if you are signed to a long-term lease. Working from your home allows you to hire more people or fewer people, or simply work longer or shorter hours to right-size your business operations.

3. Deduction of Home Costs on Income Taxes

The tax benefits of operating a home office can be lucrative. If your situation qualifies, you can deduct a portion of your home's expenses, such as mortgage interest, property taxes, utilities and repairs and maintenance, against your business income.

To qualify, your home office must be your principal place of business and you can only deduct the proportionate amounts of the total expense which are directly related to your business.

Although you cannot create a loss with your home office expenses, you can carry them forward to future tax years if you do not have enough business income to use them up in the current year. (Running your own business has both personal and financial perks.

4. Flexibility of Working Hours

Being able to work at night or first thing in the morning is a great boon for those entrepreneurs who are juggling children or other obligations. Mobile phones, faxes and email allow you to interact with your customers and suppliers at any time of the day or night. You can more easily accommodate customers in different time zones and kids' school schedules.

5. Reduction in Overhead Costs

Working from a home-based office keeps your overhead costs low as you are not renting office space or phones or paying for office utilities. The zero commute also saves money on gas and wear and tear on your car. The reduction in fixed costs allows you to be more flexible in your pricing decisions than competitors who must cover those types of costs. You can choose to either give more favorable quotes or keep the same pricing as your competition and have a healthier bottom line.

6. Allows You to Test Out Business Ideas

More than 50% of all new businesses fail. If you have had to put money out for office space and other fixed costs right off the bat, a start-up failure can be costly. Working from a home office allows you to test out a new business without a lot of overhead. This way, you can determine its viability before investing a lot of money.

The Bottom Line

Starting a business from your home allows you many freedoms and flexibilities to grow your business at your own pace. It also saves money on many fronts, which helps during the often-lean start up years.

You can use these advantages as a prospecting tool; this tool is always rejection free.

Everybody wants to save their money on taxes while making more money, you can approach people using this approach who are dead set against MLM.

It's almost forces everyone to ask you for the details about how you can help them to save on their taxes.

You can also create a funded proposal and distribute it to attract more and more serious prospects.

You can calculate your tax report by Rocket Recruiting

9. How to pitch in BNI or Networking Groups over and over again without being thrown out completely?

This is the best way to leverage the power of networking groups.

BNI is the largest privately held Networking group.

Don't go to any chapter and start pitching your opportunity. You will get kicked out.

Meet people outside the chapter. Encourage your team-mates to join other chapters in the same city or different cities.

Go to chapter co-ordinator and ask him" **Would you introduce me to 3 most well-networked people in your group?"**

Biggest Mistakes to avoid

1. Pitch your opportunity

    When you go to any BNI chapter, don't lead with your opportunity. First get to know these people, ask them open ended questions. Be interested in them.

2. Don't talk to everyone

    Pick 1 or 2 people and get to know them. They will introduce you to the right people.

3. Don't be a guest at every other place

    You can try 2 -3 different chapters but don't be the person who is attending every other chapter for free. They will ban you forever.

60 Second Commercial

There are 4 ways to do commercial (or present your products)

1. Explain products

2. Tell product stories

3. Testimonials

4. Show your product and tell people, allow them to experience it.

10. How to make money even when distributors quit?

This is one of the best strategies for getting more & more referrals from existing customers and it's also one of the ways to make money when your distributors quit or customers who don't want to actively participate in the business.

You have to use this on your existing customers. Don't use it on anybody else.

There are two types of customers.

1. Customers who love your product and share the benefits with the world.

2. Customers who love your product but they are not interested in building the business.

This referral way teaches you how to get referrals from second type of people without offending them. Most people don't approach their customers for referrals out of fear.

Advantages of referral

1. Easier to set up appointment

   All conditions being equal, people will do business with people they know, like and trust. It's called "borrowed influence"

2. Price is not an issue

   "When you sell based on price, you are a commodity. When you sell based on value, you are a resource."

3. Easier to complete the transaction

How to ask for referrals?

Use this *referral bridge approach* so both of you and your customer feels comfortable.

Let's say you are talking to one of your customers Paul. Note: Don't try to mimic the script but make sure you use all the principles mentioned in it.

"John, I am in the process of expanding my referral business, I find it's useful to partner with friends and customers such as you. Can we take a few quick minutes and run past the names of some other people I might also be able to help?"

11. How to get paid for prospecting even when nobody signs up with you?

A MLM funded proposal is the process of selling an inexpensive, but extremely useful product on the "front end" and then "back-ending" the real product or service (opportunity).

Using a Funded Proposal to offer solutions on the front end to help other marketers puts you in a position to do that.

You will then build a qualified list of leads who will possibly join your MLM.

e.g. This book is a funded proposal. You can sell this book to create your own funded proposal.

Also it's a great system to get paid to hear "NO"

So how to create funded proposal?

1. Funded Proposal to attract Network Marketing prospects

2. Funded Proposal to attract Non-network Marketing prospects

The concept of funded proposal is derived from Direct Marketing Principle

"Market information, not products."

If you sell a product or service, you should lead with information about solving problems, not information about the product or service itself.

Nobody who bought a drill wanted a drill. They wanted a hole.

What this means for you is that instead of providing information about drills, you should deliver information about making holes. You'll get a lot more prospects – with fewer literature collectors – and build more rapport with prospective customers that way.

This is massively huge.

This is NOT an afterthought. It is an entire shift in strategic direction that can create fantastically effective results.

1. Funded Proposal for existing network marketers: Sell this book, to create funded proposal or you can use this system

   Magnetic Sponsoring

2. Funded Proposal for non-MLMers : Create a resource which is an information resource. e.g. Create a book on "*How to pay less in taxes while making more money* " or " *Why it's the best time to start home-based business*" or " *Do you still want to buy franchise, think again* ?"

   Basically, you can come up with a lot of such topics, which indirectly suggests to your prospects that, how they can benefit more after reading your report and ask you how they can accomplish their goals through either not buying any franchise or saving more in taxes.

12. How to create prospect-inhaling blog on the budget?

Blogging is one of the best ways to get leads. Although it's not a short term strategy, a long term strategy. You can't be solely dependent on blogging for getting prospects. You should use it as an additional tool.

Few steps:

Register a domain name. Hostgator or GoDaddy or Namecheap

Install Wordpress on it.

Install theme of your choice.

You can outsource the whole process from www.odesk.com or www.elance.com

Plugins to use

1. SEO Pressor or Easy WP SEO : SEO

2. Premium List Magnet or Popup Domination or Welcome Gate : Optin Form

3. Pretty Link or Ninja Affiliate : Affiliate Link Cloaker

4. Akismet : Spam Blocking

5. Google Analytics

6. Google XML sitemap

7. WP Social Share : Share buttons

8. WP Touch : Mobile browsing

How to come up with content ideas?

1. Write about your experience or your upline's experience.

2. Whenever you attend the training, take notes and write on the topic?

3. Talk to your uplines, downlines, crosslines the problems they are facing and help them to overcome them and write an article about it.

4. Interview your successful upline (audio, video or text), put it on your website as an article.

5. Read blogs in MLM niche to find out what topics others write on, make a note of them and then write an article about it.

How to make more money if nobody signs up with you?

Whenever you end your article, always end it with funded proposal offer like Magnetic Sponsoring

You can either come up with your own product or promote other offer (Magnetic Sponsoring) or any other offer you find suitable. This is a generic offer and so people reading your blogs will obviously take a look at it. Make sure you promote right products at the end, if you write an article on sponsoring more people, promote Blackbelt Recruiting offer.)

The most important thing in blogging is consistency and congruency. Make sure you blog at regular intervals.

Become a member at www.betternetworker.com , it's a platform where around 1,00,000 Networkers are registered, so it's the perfect place for your content marketing as well as advertisements.

How to attract leads and monetize them?

Use your optin form to collect names and email ids of the people. Give them something valuable in exchange, for example "10 ways to attract more prospects" or "3 questions you should never ask to the serious prospect"

Use services like aweber or icontact for email marketing.

Email them daily or with regular intervals to keep them in follow-up.

The more tips about how to create compelling and irresistible lead magnet, how to use email marketing for fun and profits, how to get creative content ideas and much more in the Member's area.

13. How to create instant local market even when nobody knows likes and trusts you?

This method will help you to create local prospecting goldmine, even nobody in your locality loves you and everybody hates your guts.

There are two ways to create local prospects, either spend money or either spend time.

This is the creative idea to create *unlimited prospects locally* and requires a lot less money.

Before you use this method, ask yourself these three questions

1. **Would you like someone who has a job or someone who is unemployed**?

Obviously, you want someone with a job. Atleast they have money to buy your product.

2. **Would you like people who love their jobs or hate their jobs**?

Obviously, you want people who hate their jobs. They are pretty motivated.

3. **Would you like these people locally or at the places which are far away**?

Obviously, you want these people locally and exclusive to you.

So the requirements are

1. They have a job.

2. They hate their job.

3. They are local prospects.

4. They are exclusive to you.

Find the places where these people congregate. Let's say, they go to eat sandwich shop near their office, then go to the sandwich owner and say "Hey, Sandwich owner, is it OK if I give away some sandwiches and pay for them." If he says OK, then tell him, I am going to keep a fishbowl here and run a little contest, so people who buy the sandwiches will fill out the form while waiting in the line.

In fishbowl, there is a small entry form, they have to finish the sentence, enter their name, email and mobile no., so you can notify them.

"Win a sandwich, all you have to do is finish the sentence "I hate my job because.."

Collect the names after a week, declare the winner.

You have information of people who hate their jobs and why they hate their jobs, so if you pay $5 for 100 such names, it costs 5 cents per each prospect.

For other 99 people, send them the message, you didn't win sandwich, but you get to win this free CD on how to fire your boss in 90 days or how to save taxes by owning a home based business or your product/service demo.

Give your name, address; I will mail it to you.

They are already entered for the next week contest.

14. How to defang loud and obnoxious prospects and making them beg you to show your plan?

The people who have already burned their hands in MLM before are sometimes non-receptive, arrogant and overly negative but there is a method to sign up these people.

The reason it's easy because their best defense is acting loud, arrogant, and noisy.

And many people get easily offended by their arrogance.

What you have to take into account at this stage is that _their arrogance is their only weapon_.

The principle behind this is "**Curiosity overrides Programming**"

So when next time you encounter a prospect like that instead of arguing with him and telling him how good your product/business is, ask him

"You must be having a horrible experience with your previous company, upline, friend." And stop and just listen."

He will start telling you more and more, listen for a few minutes. Let him scream, yell and let his anger subside. It's like letting air out of hot air balloon. The longer he will talk, the mellower he will become, making selling a lot easier. Continue asking question.

Note down all his pain points, all hot buttons to sell him. Ask him then why did you sign up with him/company? He will tell you all the reasons, then note them down. Ask him how someone sold him the last opportunity and learn how he overcame all of his objections.

Now after you hear all the answers, he will most probably ask you what you have got or which company you are talking about. Then start takeaway approach.

Don't act like every other network marketer.

Use all those words he used to sell him, if he has used the word "risky", and then say "I know, it can be very risky for you at this moment, it's not the right time for you." Make him beg you to ask you about your company and compensation plan and while presenting repeat all the phrases he used and then you have eager prospect willing to give you money.

15. How to create instant rapport without using any manipulative tactics and phony gimmicks?

The ability to quickly make a connection with prospects from all walks of life is an extremely valuable skill. While some appear to be "naturals" at it, others struggle.

The good news is: it's a skill that _can be learned_.

If you don't connect as well with prospects as you'd like to, know you're not alone.

There are many who struggle with it, but you can become very accomplished the more people you speak to. Three-ways with your upline can help a lot. Over the period of time, you'll internalize some of the subtle things your upline does that works so well and naturally start doing it too.

Personal growth is a big bonus that comes from working in this industry, and the more you do it, the better (and more comfortable) working with cold market prospects you'll become.

Here are some tips for instantly connecting with your prospects:

1. **Ask prospects questions, and really listen to their answers** (not just what they say, but how they say it). You'll pick up a wealth of information that'll help you establish greater rapport.

2. **When your prospect says something you want to explore further, probe deeper** by saying "John, tell me more about that", or "why do you feel that way?"

3. **Match your prospect's style**. If your prospect is a slow speaker, adjust your speech to match. If he or she has a quick and efficient pace, again, match your pace to theirs. This is subtle, but it goes a long way to establishing a strong connection.

4. When your prospect comes back with a legitimate objection, agree with them. (More about this in Pattern Interrupt Close)This can be very disarming as they often are expecting you to argue the point. Instead agree with it, then re-frame it and include a solution.

For instance: Your prospect says: "I'm not sure I know enough people who'd want to join me in a business like this".

Your response. "You know what Joe, you're right, if you're like most of the successful people on our team, you probably don't. That's why we give you some highly effective marketing strategies for making new connections in your local market that can expand your business even more rapidly."

Wow. Talk about powerful. "Joe" was expecting you to argue with her and say something like: "Oh no Joe, you know way more people than you think you do" but instead of arguing you agreed with her and validated what she already knows to be true and you weaved a powerful solution in with your response that let her know that "you know" how to help her be successful.

This approach is highly effective for building trust and rapport and can substantially increase your sponsoring success. Just be sure and use it with the right prospects or else you may end up sponsoring people who you really don't want in your business.

16. How to melt prospect's resistance?

Why Story Telling is required?

Because by weaving the ideas and beliefs that underpin your business presentation into the golden threads of story, you can sell to people without them feeling like they are being sold.

1. They can cast away their irrational fears and give the arguments embedded in your story a fair hearing.

2. They can then act confidently in their own best interests by investing in you and your offerings.

This kind of soft selling is crucial in today's MLM arena, where potential prospects are more cynical, suspicious, and resistant to your pitch than ever before.

A well-crafted story is truly hypnotic.

Through story, they can see things that were invisible to them before. They can feel new sensations that empower them to take actions that were previously impossible.

Story selling is powerful because it speaks the natural language of our species. Its structure is natural and easy, allowing you to create a heart-to-heart connection between you and your prospects, thereby bypassing the skepticism and cynicism of adulthood to a large degree.

We are integrating our storytelling into a larger pattern of persuasion. Our stories are like tools that we can use to overcome challenges and close more prospects.

Seizing and maintaining the attention of our prospects is certainly one of those challenges. If they're not with you, engaged in your presentation, you can hardly expect them to sign up with you or buy your product.

There is a defensive blockade that people put up against persuasion that stories naturally disarm. People will listen to you when you tell them a story to see where it leads, while they blatantly reject the idea of hearing some dry facts.

If you tell your story well, your prospects want to know if the hero of the story will get what he wants. They want to know how he will get it. And they want to know how the experience will change his life and his character for the better.

So you weave the facts, features, and benefits of your product or service into the fabric of the hero's story. And your prospects are held in enchantment until the yarn is unravelled and because they are being entertained while they are being informed; closing ratio goes through the roof.

The stories allow you to paint vivid mental pictures in your prospect's imaginations, that's why they are inherently believable.

The unconscious mind literally can't tell the difference between a real and an imagined experience, so the premise or conclusion buried in the sub-text of a story (the hidden meaning) is much more easily accepted than a straight recitation of fact.

Stories are fabulous teaching tools as well. They allow you to present complex or new ideas to your prospects clearly, giving them the confidence and assurance to move ahead.

Storytelling is demonstration, it shows rather tells, forcing you to avoid abstraction.

The mind thinks in pictures. And when you abstract an argument, you leave it up to your prospects to create their own mental imagery.

Often they will not understand your abstractions well enough to create those images. Often they will not care to do the work.

A well told story solves these age-old selling challenges. Your pitch becomes entertaining, believable, and crystal clear to your audience and sell happens.

You can come up with story of your experience if it's compelling enough, your product experience story, you can tell the story of someone who has been through all the challenges and has overcome them, and you can talk about product testimonials of other people.

Whatever you find compelling enough, share with your prospects.

If you want to retail your products, tell product story.

If you want to sell your business opportunity, tell success story of yours or someone else.

Make sure, your average prospect will buy into the story and can relate to it.

17. How to stop objection dead in their tracks by using this weird NLP trigger?

This is not a very famous technique but it works like gangbusters if you use it properly. If used properly and on the right prospects, you can see the amazing results.

Don't use it on all the people otherwise you will end up sponsoring the people you may not want in your business.

This technique is a part of NLP, so some people might know about it.
It's basically used to re-frame prospects objection. You can use it to instantly defang loud and obnoxious prospects.

When you are talking with the prospect, when the decision of buying comes, prospects defences are high and at the same moment, the prospects are expecting that you will start argue with them but if you use it properly it can drastically reduce their defences and their focus immediately shifts back on you.

It can be used to turn the tables on the prospects. They immediately start seeing you in a different role i.e. from a Salesman to a Consultant.

If you use calculated pattern interrupts, it can be very disarming for the prospects and it can throw them off balance.

Basically use them to weed out tire kickers and fence sitters. It's basically saying the unexpected.

For example, if a prospect asks you

"Why should I join your company?"

Don't get into argumentative mode but instead say like this.

"Actually you shouldn't."

Take a pause and then say "Not until you ask yourself some hard questions." and then go into consultant mode.

If a prospect asks you

"How long the company is going to last?"

Don't say "The Company is great. It is doing xxxxx turnover every single year. It's on top of charts. Its product is so unique. Blah Blah."

Instead say

"I don't know, I mean the company is doing xxx turnover, xx no of customers, with background of xxx, under the stellar leadership of xxxx, I don't know what is going to happen, but what do you think?"

If a prospect asks you

"I need to think about it."

Don't go into convincing mode. Many people after hearing this response go into that mode. Instead say something like this

"I think you really should."

And then take a pause and then say

"Let me ask you something, how many times you will allow your fears to hold you back?"

If the person understands it, he will take the decision then and there itself and if someone doesn't get it, let them go.

18. How to make your prospects nodding their head during entire presentation and even ready to buy when you ask for the sale?

This method works extremely well and will guarantee to double your closing ratio almost overnight.

Trial close is like letting your prospect nod his head or say "YES" several times in the presentation by asking him particular type of questions.

You can use it in videos, live webinars and in 1 on 1 presentation.

So next time, use some of these questions and see the response going up.

Use few of these phrases in your presentations at right times to make prospects nod their heads.

1. So are you guys excited for this?

2. Can you see how this will benefit your health?

3. Do you want a free sample of it?

4. Are you ready to take the next step?

5. Do you want to be the next success story?

6. Would you like to know how this can shortcut your way to success?

7. Are you ready to get started today?

8. Are you ready to create passive source of income?

You can create specific questions according to your opportunity/ products/ services. Questions can be different depending upon whether you are on live webinar, video, 1 on 1 presentation.

Insert these trial closes every time when you finish explaining a testimonial, concept, social proof.

You will see whooping increase in your closing ratio.

19. How to use Tony Robbins' closing formula for your advantage?

This strategy is used by many famous speakers including Tony Robbins for closing big ticket sales.

Test closing is hugely powerful.

It works like this

After you find out prospect's pain, say:

"In your opinion, do you feel, think, or believe that this would help [your problem]?"

If someone says they don't have the time to join your business, ask: **"In your opinion, do you feel, think, or believe that this would help create more time for you?"**

What you're doing is building an emotional benefit bank in their head by doing these test closes.

This is you testing the temperature of the prospect to see if you should move forward.

You could start with: **"In your opinion, do you feel, think, or believe that this would help you [raise the money you need for your new car / your wedding / your new home]?"**

Then, ask: **"What would that be worth to you?"**

Next, challenge them. **"Now, are you just saying that or do you really believe that this home business will really do all that?"**

Then ask this million dollar question: **"If you were to join now, what would be the best benefit to you joining?"**

Test the temperature of the prospect.

At any stage, they can give you resistance, and you can roll right back and say: "**Oh, I'm sorry, just from the way you were talking it sounded as if you were ready to join.**"

"**What did you like about what you saw?**"

If they are positive, say this phrase: "**Sounds to me like you're ready to join.**"

Prospect: **You know what? I really like this business because it looks to me like I would save money on taxes, I paid so much in taxes last year.**

You: **Well, in your opinion, do you feel that having a home based business would help with your taxes?**

Prospect: Well, yeah, absolutely.

 You: Well, what would that be worth to you?

Prospect: I don't know. Probably about thousand dollars a month.

You: Just curious. Are you just saying that or do you actually believe that? Do you know that this would actually save you money?

Prospect: Absolutely.

Now make use of this Rocket Recruiting App to help your prospects to see how much they are saving.

Advanced Objection Handling

Take the objection. Repeat it into a question. You cannot answer objections, but you can answer questions.

Prospect: I think these products are overpriced.

You: **I'm sure you have a reason for saying that. What's the reason?**

Prospect: **Nobody makes money in MLM.**

You: **I'm sure you have a reason for saying that. What's the reason?**

Listen.

Are you doing the hard work, or are they? Let them finish, then say this: "**Suppose I was able to satisfy that concern. In your opinion, do you feel you would want to move forward?**"

By the way, "In your opinion, do you feel ..." is a hypnotic phrase as well as *a test close*, notice that there is also an embedded direct command in the question. "Move forward." This is a great combination. They may stop you. They may say that they'd be willing to move forward if you could address that question.

Then ask:"**In spite of [this objection], isn't the real question: 'Is it possible for you to get more benefits than you are investing? Isn't that the real question? That it's going to be worth more than you are spending? Isn't that the real question?**"

What if they say they **don't have any money.**

That is rarely the true case. Rarely will it be the case that they actually don't have enough money. What they are saying is that they don't see this as being beneficial enough to them for them to spend the money.

You want them to think: "**Hang on for a moment. This would really help me. This is beneficial. I want to invest money into this,**" and they see more hurt in buying than pleasure.

Here is one response to that objection:

You: **I appreciate that you don't have any money, and** [not "but". Don't say. Say and from now on, not but. Don't say: "I appreciate that, but ..." because when you say but it negates them. People don't appreciate that.] **in spite of not having any money, isn't the real question how you can start enjoying the benefits now, without waiting for longer?**

Them: I like it, but I don't have any money.

You: If you had worked out the money, what would have been the biggest factor that would have helped you to come up with the money?

It's amazing what solutions they will come up with from that. There's also a embedded direct command in that one: **come up with the money**. This will get you some details on how serious they are and how you can proceed.

20. How to make super irresistible offer to your prospect which is almost impossible for him to pass up or too costly to pass up?

This is a revolutionary concept you can use to sell your business opportunity or your products through your own website/ advertisement/ free report or funded proposal.

It's like creating such an irresistible offer that any right prospect can't refuse it.

e.g. You have created a free report on how you can earn more while saving more money in taxes.

At the end of the report, say something like this for CTA(Call To Action)

"Would you like me to show how you can instantly start saving taxes while making more money with a proven home based business model and marketing plan which breaks even almost instantly when you start ?

I am happy to help you calculate how much money you can save on taxes every year, earn more money, start your own home based business at the same time.

This way you can finally be able to start saving more money without much hassle and wasting your valuable time.

There is no charge for this and there is no obligation of any kind.

I offer this service because I am home business consultant and tax advisor and there is a good probability that I can help you achieve the same.

So if you find value in the help I give you, you might want me to save your taxes.

With that, I am not offering you a sales pitch in disguise.

I promise not to pressure or pester you in any way at all.

In fact, if you feel I have wasted even one second of your time, let me know and I'll xxxxxx(say what you are going to do)."

Then use takeaway.

"But before I go further, you need to know that, I can't help everyone, I can only be help to people

1. *Who are paying $1000 in taxes*

2. *Who travels atleast once in a year (preferably outside the country)*

Schedule a planning session with me.

My office no is XXXXXX."

This is just the example of how you can use collaborative close to attract more qualified prospects. You don't necessarily have to copy this template; you can modify it according to whatever offer you give to the prospects.

21. Objection Obliteration Formula: How to dodge 10,000 pounds of heavy duty objections with 200 ounces of energy?

Objections are of two types.

1. Real and genuine objection

2. Smokescreen objection

You should know which objection your prospect is having before you proceed further.

If objection is real and genuine there is a different way to handle them and if objection is smokescreen, there is a different way to handle them.

Objections are a good thing. A sign that your prospect is thinking seriously about your opportunity. They're either:

a) your prospects way of "slowing down" the process so as not to make a mistake and jump into something they don't understand

   OR

b) a test. That's right, experienced networkers (or savvy prospects) will sometimes launch objections at you to see how (and if) you can handle them.

Why? Because they know they'll be ask questions too, and they're interested in one of two things:

1) Are there good answers for those questions OR

2) Do you know what you're doing? Can you answer the hard questions? Are you the type of person who's going to be able to help them get to where they want to go.

Objection #1: How much money are you making?

This is generally not a genuine objection, it's a smokescreen objection. It's also a bad question. The reason is , it proceeds from the assumption that whatever you're doing (or not doing) is how it's going to go for them too.

What your prospect really wants to know is whether you have the real opportunity, one that is legitimate and viable, one that people can really make decent income in.

Insincere prospects are simply looking for an excuse not to participate. Disqualify these people at the early stage.

Your response back to the serious prospect is "It's not about what I make, it's about what you're going to make (or not make)".

Objection #2: Let me think it over.

Smokescreen objection again.

This one's very common and it's important that you have a good read on your prospect (which you should by the time it comes up at the end of the process).

Best Response: You know John, with what you've shared with me about (repeat his reasons why) and the opportunity you now have to do something about it. What is there really to think about?

The point of this response is to ferret out any remaining objections that they've not yet voiced. If they have them, deal with them and then sign them up.

If they're silent at this point (i.e. can't come up with any), you can usually say (with a smile)

Right. So why don't we go ahead and get you started ?

Now if instead they come back with.. "I don't rush into things, I just want to think about it", here's where you have to read your prospect.

If they're just delaying because they have trouble making decisions, respond by saying "John, you're not one of those "tire kickers" are you? No?

That's good, then let's move forward and get you plugged in and rolling.

Some prospects are quite serious, yet their personality just needs time to make that decision. This is a judgment call on your part. If they legitimately need time,

You can respond with:

Tell you what John, I want you take a day or two and go through the information I gave you again carefully. When join, I want you excited to be coming aboard our team.

I don't want you coming in with your fingers crossed behind your back that you're not making some big mistake.

Take your time, go through it and let's talk on (set date & time).

Objection #3: I'm not sure if my wife will let me do this.

Smokescreen objection.

John, let me ask you a question. Did your wife give you permission to stay in a job that's keeping you broke?

When you say it though, you have to be perfectly silent afterwards and not say anything till they respond.

Some of them will say "You're right, let's do it."

Other times, people are like, yeah, I know, you're right. I still got to ask her.

These are generally not the people you want in your business anyway so just tell them

Best Response:

"That's ok John. I'm really only interested in working with people who are driven, decisive and serious. That's doesn't sound like you so I'm going to go ahead and let you go".

Objection #4: How much will I make?

Genuine or Smokescreen.

Be honest. The answer is:

Best Response: "I don't know".

Tell them that. Let them know what they make is ultimately up to them.

You can tell people flat out that you can't promise they'll make a dime.

People respect honest, so be honest. They may go on to huge success or they mail fail.

It's up to them. There's risk in any business. What you're offering isn't a guarantee, it's an opportunity.

If they're looking for a "sure thing", then tell them they're not cut out to be an entrepreneur. All businesses have risk attached.

Objection #5: Can you guarantee me that I'll make money?

Best Response:

NO, but I can guarantee you this, if you keep doing what you've been doing over the past few years you'll likely stay stuck where you are today, few years from now and is that really where you want to be?

Again, you're being honest and you're pointing out something people often fail to consider: that there is risk in doing nothing as well. The risk that if they "do nothing", then nothing will change.

The right people will not want to risk doing nothing. Those are the people you want to be working with.

Objection#6: The products are expensive.

When you sell on the basis of value, you are a resource. When you sell on the basis of price, you are a commodity.

If they say, the products are expensive. You can ask them compared to what.

Most of the people become silent after you ask them this question; they don't have any good answer.

They might say, well the entry price is higher, then you can say "It means, if you see more value and more returns after signing up, then you would not have this objection anyways, right ?

Serious prospect will say "Yes", explain the value proposition to them and sign them up otherwise let them go.

Objection#7: I don't think I have the time.

Smokescreen objection.

Your prospect doesn't see any possible returns after investing time in your opportunity/products.

Tell them

"Exactly John, it's not about having more time, it's about creating."

Objection#8: I don't like to sell.

Genuine or Smokescreen objection.

Ask him, "John, do you like to sell?" to which obvious reply from john is NO.

Then say "Good, because this isn't a selling business. It's is a coaching business. It's about working with a team to help inspire & create success in others."

Objection#9: My friend/spouse/parents said, these things don't work.

Genuine or Smokescreen objection.

If you find it's genuine, ask him "John, you sure have a reason to say this, tell me more about it."

If it's smokescreen objection, then say

"Really? How much money does your friend make? If the response is a decent dollar figure (and it's usually not), then respond with: "great, and he (or she) work for themselves and aren't slaving away making someone else rich, right?" And finish it with: "Point is, why on earth you would take financial advice from your broke friend? You're kidding me, right?"

If they don't "get it" immediately after you say this – they're gone & you're on to your next prospect.

22. How to make prospect sign up only at higher price point and almost afraid to join at lower price point?

This is the strategy used by _used car salesmen_ to sell their cars but the problem with the car salesmen is that they are _extremely dishonest_. They manipulate and lie to people. You obviously don't want to do that, so don't use this tactic with dishonesty.

This tactic will only work, if your company has different levels of entry price.

So if you have shown a presentation to a prospect and he is ready to start the business but the problem is, the person is keen to start only on the lowest entry level because he thinks it's too risky to put a lot of money upfront or he thinks let him earn first before he buys into higher price level.

So the exact point to use this is when you know you have qualified buyer, he has more money to invest. What you can do at this moment is to restate him obvious benefits of joining at higher price which may include _more payout, more benefits, faster results whatever_ but also state that if he buys into lower price stuff, then there is higher likelihood that he will fail because when the stakes are low, it's very easy for people to quit. That's why so many people quit MLM.

What you can also do is give him examples of people in your downlines, uplines or crosslines who quit the business because they started at lowest entry point and by doing that you are not exactly lying or manipulating here because if he starts at lower price, there are much more chances that he is not going to last long but if he comes with the higher stake, there is more likelihood that he won't fizzle out after some small or big challenges.

23. The biggest duplication lie busted once and for all. The lie is "It doesn't matter what works, it does matter what duplicates."

Myth about Duplication

"**People are not duplicable... systems are**."

And more than likely so has something like this: "Look at the things you do and ask yourself: 'Is this duplicable', Can everyone on my team follow the system I'm using?"

99% of networkers accept these statements as indisputable truths.

They're repeated tens of thousands of times by their upline leaders but that doesn't make them true.

In fact, the 1% who don't blindly subscribe & apply such clichés, often out earn the 99% who do.

Crazy but true.

What happens is people become so concerned about being duplicable, they become highly inflexible in their approach.

As a result, they struggle, and often never crack $3000 a month let alone $10,000/mo or more.

So... the next time someone hits you with a cliché regarding duplication, remember this:

It's OK to do and try things that aren't 100% duplicable.

And while you're at it, also remember this:

NO one system is ever going to be right for everybody on your team. You could have the perfect internet driven system and there will still be people who can't (or won't) use it.

You can have the perfect system for conducting meetings, and your downline who lives and works in NYC and rides the subway to and from work day after day may have trouble building with it.

Don't be afraid to do what works for you.

Example: say you're really good with SEO marketing and generating prospects online, and are using a system to attract serious prospects that's not duplicable.

Are you doomed to failure because no one will ever be able to duplicate you?

The "herd" will be quick to argue: "yes." "You'll never do it alone" they'll cry... "your system's not duplicable."

But is "the herd" right? NO -- they're not!

While it's true you can't "do it alone," it's also true you won't have to.

Picture this: using your SEO system you attract and sponsor 27 sharp, professional realtors over the next 90 days.

Will you/they fail because they can't "duplicate you" and prospect with your SEO system?

Listen, just because they came in through the net doesn't mean they have to build the exact same way.

What if instead you work with them on how to mine their rolodex/ iphone/ blackberry etc. and getting their business in front of other professionals with whom they already have a business relationship, and then continue to network through those people to uncover other professionals who might be good candidates for their business? Help them do that, and they may soon be out-recruiting you.

I've recruited many people over the years who because of their experience, background and strengths end up building very differently than I do.

No one system will ever be a perfect match for everyone -systems are tools, and if your goal is to build a substantial long-term business, don't be afraid to have several.

The secret is to remain flexible, work with people as individuals, and get them plugged into the right system that capitalizes on their individual strengths.

And by the way, if you adopt a flexible style you'll also attract and recruit more people into your business.

Over the years I've watched people build remarkable success on my teams using a variety of different building styles and systems including meetings (yes meetings), PPC, funded proposals, SEO, etc. etc. etc.

One more thing.

When I started out in networking a decade ago, I attempted to duplicate the style of some of the most successful networkers of the time, top earners / recruiters who were enjoying immense success in our industry.

You know what? It worked. I didn't stop being me... I just grew a little.

I became more outgoing, more confident and began attracting leaders, serious players and builders. My business took off.

I continued to develop that style and ultimately made it unique to me.

So to some degree, people ARE duplicable. Over the years, I've had a number of people duplicate my style and create success too.

Bottom line: don't buy into clichés. And don't be too quick to follow the herd. Sometimes, it pays to do your own thinking. It sure has for me.

See you soon,

M.W. (Name not disclosed to maintain privacy)

This article is written by Gentleman goes by initials M.W. who build the team of more than 10,000 distributors in less than 24 months with average start-up costs were $800.

24. Resources

MLM Prospecting for Introverts

http://www.amazon.com/dp/B00JJ65NIU/

How To Become MLM Closing Monster ?

http://www.amazon.com/dp/B00JJ3UGVW/

How to Double, Triple even Quadruple Your Closing Ratio Practically Overnight ?

http://www.amazon.com/dp/B00JIV3M48/

Blackbelt Recruiting

http://www.rebelmlm.com/bbr

Pro Blog Academy

http://www.rebelmlm.com/problogacademy

www.ingramcontent.com/pod-product-compliance
Lightning Source LLC
Chambersburg PA
CBHW051815170526

45167CB00005B/2026